Putting Out the Fire

Nurturing Mind, Body & Spirit
in the First Week of Loss

Claire M. Schwartz

Helian Press Books
2015

Text Copyright © 2015
Helian Press Books
All Rights Reserved

Cover Design & Layout: Angie Ayala
Typesetting: Scribe Inc.

ISBN: 978-0-9963099-2-9

No part of this book may be reproduced in any form or by any electronic or mechanical means, including information storage and retrieval systems, without written permission from the author, except in the case of a reviewer, who may quote brief passages embodied in critical articles or in a review.

Trademarked names appear throughout this book. Rather than use a trademark symbol with every occurrence of a trademarked name, names are used in an editorial fashion, with no intention of infringement of the respective owner's trademark.

The information in this book is distributed on an "as is" basis, without warranty. Although every precaution has been taken in the preparation of this work, neither the author nor the publisher shall have any liability to any person or entity with respect to any loss or damage caused or alleged to be caused directly or indirectly by the information contained in this book.

Dedication

In loving memory of my beautiful mother

Eleanor Delia Lipkin (1930–1995)

Pianist, Nature Girl, Free Spirit
Broken Heart and Soul in Pain

Our paths crossed in times of turmoil
You left yours before that could be righted
Now I walk mine in a light we never got to share
But you are in my thoughts always

Acknowledgements

No journey is undertaken alone—not nearly....
In my travels and travails, I must thank the following:

The Dearly Departed

My mother, Eleanor Lipkin, whose sacrifices are lost to time and history—but not to me.

My stepmother, Eva Klein, for her courage, her grace and her spirit.

My father, Toma Schwartz—in spite of our differences.

All the others I lost from 2010–2012—Annemarie, Saratoga, Rob, Margaret Ann, Fred; community; time; health; opportunities....

Beloved Felines—Duncan, Lacey, Packer, Chalice.

My Teachers

Margaret Ann Case (1953–2010), Reiki Master Teacher and Guide, who started me on the healer's path.

Frans Steine of the International House of Reiki, Guide and Mentor, for his peerless insight and generous wisdom.

Acknowledgements

Drs. Sharon & Glenn Livingston of the International Coach Certification Academy, for their brilliance and kindness, plain and simple.

David Schwing, LCSW—whose openness and depth were the catalysts for my growth and understanding of myself.

John Chancellor—my coach and southern gentleman.

All the kind folks who patiently and diligently read various drafts of this book and gave me invaluable feedback.

My patient, loving Other Half, Mark Zdziarski, who believes in me when things get rough.

And my friends far and wide who have been my rock and salvation more times than I care to count—Jon, Jean, Nanci, Ann, Mary, Steve, Patricia, Michael . . . more than I can count. And to David, Ethan, Beth, et al, for their boundless support after Mom died.

You stunning human beings—I would have been dead long ago without you. . . .

From the bottom of my heart—I thank you.

Table of Contents

Dedication — iii
Acknowledgements — v
Preface — ix

Introduction — 1
Self-Care and Love — 9
Taking Care of Business — 19
Behavior of Others — 25
Time & The Longer Term — 47
Celebrating Your Loved One and Yourself — 57
Conclusion — 63

Biography — 69
Resources — 71

Preface

We all experience loss—and yet Western culture does a rather poor job of equipping us to cope with loss—of any kind. Buddhism and The Stoic Greek Philosophers teach us that loss is an inevitable part of life. Death in particular can seem to come out of nowhere—the phone rings, a long struggle with illness ends, and reality knocks the wind from your lungs and your heart begins to pound. We are in shock and in denial that this could ever happen. But it happens to all of us—many times.

When you suffer a major loss—a death, property loss, health change, job termination, a divorce—life can suddenly seem unbearable. The grief can be severe—it can come in waves and there seems to be no hope. And our lack of preparation only deepens the pain we experience.

At those times, you do not need well-meaning, but empty, words from friends, family members or even clergy. You need some <u>real</u> help. The first few days after a death can be especially and uniquely difficult. People

Preface

may tell you that the pain eventually goes away. But before you can worry about coping long-term, you must focus on getting through the extremely painful and challenging demands upon you in the short term. That is the purpose of this book.

In the following pages, you will find powerful & effective ways to help you endure and survive those first hours and days. After you have Put Out The Fire of the immediate shock and stress, then you can address longer term issues, and seek healing, reconciliation and peace in your spirit once again.

Introduction

The beginning is the most important part of the work.
Plato

Hello and Welcome

If you have picked up this book, it's because you are hurting—you may have just lost someone close to you and you don't know what to do. Your head is spinning and the earth is not solid beneath your feet. You have a million things to do, but you can barely hold a thought in your head. And your heart is broken into so many pieces, you feel like it will never be whole again.

I know—I've been there—more times than I can count. But I can tell you it WILL get better and I'm here to teach you what to do in the first hours and days following the death of a loved one, to address the immediate issues that need to be taken care of while your heart is aching, and to get you on the road to healing, to finding a New Normal as you go forward.

Many of us have experienced loss early in life, at much too tender an age to be able to comprehend it, much less know how to cope with or heal the avalanche of emotions that rain down on a small head and heart. Children's emotional needs may have been dismissed, or they may have been told to "be strong" or "be a big girl," or "boys don't cry." So one may have reached adulthood without ever really processing the grief from that loss. Plus you may have internalized our culture's discomfort with grieving and the unhelpful advice that often surfaces.

Then as an adult (the intended audience of this book), with all of those "lessons" firmly implanted in our psyches, when loss happens, we are just in shock. And while there are many resources (of varying quality and use) out there for handling grief, there is nothing that tells you what to do in the first minutes and days of the process, when we are in a different kind of distress—our hearts are devastated—the mind goes blank—and there are a million things that need your attention NOW. What do I do?

There are no easy answers—and this book is not a place where you will find "feel good" fluff that doesn't work, or cultural myths of "what to do" that actually make you feel worse. This is for you, the Griever—the person who has <u>just</u> suffered the loss. It is about your healing, your peace of mind and your sanity, to help you get through those first difficult moments. And for that, you deserve some truths.

So right now, right this second, as you are reading this, your heart may be going a million beats a minute—let's work on that right away, to get you some immediate relief:

> I want you to take a deep breath
> Close your eyes—yes, right now
> Take a long deep breath through your nose
> Inhale for 5 seconds
> One—two—three—four—five
> Then I want you to slowly exhale through your mouth over 5 seconds
> One—two—three—four—five
> No, seriously, now that you have read this,
>   I want you to go back and do it.
> A long deep breath, in through the nose, out through the mouth
> Then do it again, in . . . . and out . . . .
> And a third time, in . . . . and out . . . .

Breath is life—and when we are suffering, we may not even be aware that we are holding it back. There's your first Truth. This release may have brought some tears of relief—that's totally fine—let it out. Go get a tissue, I'll be here when you get back.

We good? OK.

My Story

Let me give you some bare bones pieces of my story. I started losing people I loved when I was 10, with my grandmother. She was very ill from a stroke and I watched her deteriorate slowly before my eyes. The only things I was told about how to behave was to kiss her goodbye when we visited (which I hated doing, because she truly frightened me), and when she died, that I had to "be brave."

I had several more losses as I got older, but the biggest event in my life will always be the death of my mother, whom I hadn't spoken to in about two years. It came as a total shock—a phone call at midnight from my uncle, who blurted it out—"I don't know how to tell you this, but your mother has died. . . ." I got off the phone and let out a sound that only animals make and the floor fell away beneath me. Then I had to call my father and tell him (they were divorced at the time). I couldn't feel my arms or legs—I was probably in shock and should have been in the hospital. I couldn't stop shaking. My dad came, I called my boyfriend and a few friends, but I slept no more that night—and the passage of time suddenly became leaden. What happened? Who do I ask? How do I DO this?

Mom's body was in another state and had to be flown. The will left everything to me (I'm an only child), including all the decisions, about which I had less than a clue. I did the best I could with the casket, funeral, eulogy, and shiva. Then we had to fly back to her house and figure out how to move a whole houseful of stuff 600 miles away—in four days. I was 25 years old, and very immature for my age, following years of neglect, shame, fear and trauma.

In the midst of the chaos, I asked a friend of mine who had just lost her mom, how long before I feel "Normal" again? I felt outside of my body, like all this was happening to someone else, on a distant planet. I would cling to any shred of hope she could offer. But then she said, "Well, give it a year. . . ." A Year??!!? Oh, my God, that seemed like an eternity—I'll never make it through this. . . . .

In the following weeks, my whole world stopped. I couldn't work, I took a leave from my job. I essentially had a nervous breakdown—nightmares, poor sleeping and eating, too much TV and too much drinking. I was going to a therapist twice a week and it wasn't enough. I really don't remember much of that summer at all. But after three months, I switched jobs and began to come out of it. A few months later, I almost lost my Dad, too, but he survived quadruple bypass very well—and the day after his surgery, I had a lightning bolt of realization hit me—Life is *short*—what am I doing with my Life???

I knew I wanted to try my hand at acting, and the place to do that was New York. Four months later, I was there—smartest thing I ever did. I went through several career changes, got a ton of therapy, and grew myself up. I made great friends, breathed deeply from New York culture in the arts and festivals and food, and in 2008, met my future husband. The loss of my mother changed the trajectory of my life permanently, and I do not know who I would be if it hadn't happened. It's just that Mom and I were not meant to share it.

There's more of my story located on my website, www.youcanhealyourgrief.com plus posts on my blog, where I talk about my own life and losses, how I have pulled myself out of the fog of pain I had been in, and how those lessons can be useful to you. The point is that almost 20 years and dozens of losses later, I've learned a few things. And I want to share them with you, to spare you some of the years of pain and heartache I experienced, and to give you concrete, Real World things that WORK, not platitudes and promises that don't help and/or make things worse.

There are so many aspects of this complex web of emotion and heartache. Here are the categories we will examine:

- Your **Self-Care** needs, with physical, emotional and spiritual being discussed, for you cannot ignore any of these;
- The things we sometimes do to avoid our pain, and how to make wiser and healthier choices;
- **Taking Care of Business** following a loss, because there are often legal and business things that need to be done immediately (*please note, this is NOT legal advice, and you should consult an estates attorney for personal guidance*);
- **Behavior of Others**, discussing what to listen to and what to ignore when friends and family try to "help";
- The **Ten Tall Tales of Grief and Loss**™, things that are told to us immediately after a loss that can be very harmful to our healing and terribly hurtful, as well;

- ➤ Issues of **Time and the Longer Term,** which teaches you healthy ways of looking at moving forward;
- ➤ **Celebrating Your Loved One,** discussing some of the ways to honor their memory;
- ➤ The **Conclusion** covers where to go at the end of this book and how to learn the next steps of healing.

I know it feels like your life will never be the same—and you're right. Your life just changed, and that's The Truth. But you don't have to worry about all that right this second. You have a lot to do, and you may feel awash in emotion and yet numb at the same time. Let's get you some Immediate Real Help to Put Out the Fire—starting now.

Self-Care and Love

*Self-love, my liege, is not so vile
a sin as self-neglecting.*

Henry V, William Shakespeare

You are in shock, I know. That's why it is absolutely vital that you take care of yourself. It may be the furthest thing from your mind, especially because your mind feels like Swiss cheese and you cannot think straight, your heart is in shreds, and your body is numb, like there is a wool blanket around you and you cannot move. But Self-Care is part of how you will get through this.

Self-Care will also bring some flashes of Normal back into your world. With everything all sideways, you may be grateful for things that feel familiar. So here are the basics.

Food, Sleep and Medication: Do remember to eat. Even if your appetite is poor and it seems mundane. You cannot go through all this stress without fuel. Don't expect to eat perfect meals, do the best you can, but do eat something regularly.

I also believe it is perfectly ok during this immediate period to fall back onto Comfort Foods—it's just for a few days, you aren't going to make a habit of it (no, you are not). So if you want the ice cream, have the ice cream—though take it easy, only because stress can cause digestive misery! Listen to your body, it will tell you if it's annoyed with you, believe me.

Your body will also tell you when it is drained—even if you can't sleep through the night, lay your head down. Stop making decisions and worrying, and let your being rest. Sleep is essential for proper brain functioning and you need your wits about you. Naps are also a marvelous invention—just 20 minutes can work wonders.

Make sure you have a good mix of protein, carbs, water, salt and sugar—all these are vital to keep you going and make sure everything is working well. If you have a craving, listen to that. And finally, take it easy on the alcohol—I'm not being a prude, but being practical. You have things to attend to and it will muddle everything. We'll talk more about this in a bit. Until then, take it in moderation.

And finally, make sure you continue to take whatever medications you may have been prescribed. Set alarms on your phone or ask friends to remind you, but missing dosages can cause more havoc on your psyche and health.

Honor Your Emotions: It's very probable that your emotional world is in a tailspin. You may feel a million things at once or you may experience . . .

- Bursts of tears coming at unpredictable moments;
- Long stretches of sobbing (or laughter) that feel uncontrollable;
- Your face getting hot from anger;
- Your hands shaking from holding back emotions;
- Snapping at a loved one more than usual;
- Finding yourself reverting to Baby Talk;
- And more. . . .

All of these are **normal** and **understandable**, given the circumstances. And I hereby give you permission to do all of it. You may go through a whole box of tissues. A few things might get broken. It's fine, just don't cut yourself. I remember throwing a cassette case at the wall so hard, it shattered—and made a hole in the wall. I don't recommend it. . . . But I do recommend letting these emotions out, rather than bottling them up.

Every client whom I have ever had, who got emotional in my office, even to the point of sobbing uncontrollably, followed it immediately with an apology. You have **nothing** to apologize for. You are hurting and you are human.

Many of us were brought up with the adage, "Big Boys/Girls Don't Cry." Hogwash. We cry all the time, and at such painful times, expecting you to be stoic and quiet can be quite cruel. Others, including family and friends, may have preconceived ideas about what is "appropriate." But keep in mind that if it makes other people uncomfortable, that is about them, not about you. You are in control of your grieving and in these heightened first days, your feelings may be very raw. Releasing the pressure from the waves of pain inside you will release endorphins that are actually healing. Holding back that tide takes tremendous effort—you have to let it out some, so it doesn't back up. More tissues.

You may also just want to laugh—put on a cartoon, a favorite movie, do something silly. . . . Laughing is just as helpful as crying for relieving stress, and it releases the same endorphins that make you feel good. It breaks tension, creates connections and is extraordinarily healing. So go ahead—put on your best Bugs Bunny or Simpsons episode!

Of course, there are folks who react in just the opposite fashion and shut down completely. Someone recently told me that he was so eager to avoid the heartache after his mother's death, he was ready to go to work the next day. This can be normal, too—but I would caution that emotions that you are avoiding that strongly need to be attended to, and sooner rather than later. They may manifest in a sudden and less convenient time. . . .

Short Term Memory: It is a real pain that exactly when you need the most focus, your brain short-circuits. It is very common for Grievers to have trouble remembering where they put things, what they were just doing and to stay focused. For those of us in middle age, this may sound normal, but I mean MUCH more than usual. You will probably be easily distracted, may put your keys in the fridge, get lost going to regular locations . . . this is all **normal**, and again, I give you permission to be befuddled.

I know for the first few weeks after Mom died, I couldn't drive—not just because I didn't remember how, but my reaction time was way off, I was terribly distracted, I didn't know where I was going—I handed the keys to my boyfriend and said I shouldn't drive for the first week. He and various friends took turns ferrying me around town (bless their hearts).

So for remembering things, friends are a great resource—the quiet, supportive, brilliant kind are best, ones who can handle this responsibility—to help keep you on track, take you where you need to go, as well as reminding you to eat, shower, sleep, take your meds, etc. And write everything down—twice, if you need to—and make sure friends know where you wrote things.

Friends can also help with phone calls, arrangements, errands, helping you weigh options—all things that may go haywire during this immediate period. Sometimes the most important people in your life are the humans you keep close by choice, not the ones we are related to by blood.

TARPs
Temporary Actions that Relieve Pain

There are various terms for these things that we do to avoid emotional realities or things that are painful—and we are taught them at an early age. When we were hurt or upset as a child: "Don't cry, honey—have a cookie." When we hit rough waters in life: "Have a drink, it will make you feel better." And more and more common these days—"Take this, it will take all your troubles away," which could apply to uppers, downers, cocaine, heroin, ecstasy, and much more.

But it is all fake—and very dangerous.

I call them **TARPs** and here is why:

T for Temporary—some of these are fine for the moment—I am certainly guilty of taking a drink now and again. But I spent that summer in 1995 wasted—not just because I wasted the months away and don't remember them—but because I spent large chunks of it completely wasted. The thing is—when the fog clears, when you wake up the next day, the pain is still there, and often worse than before. You are just forestalling dealing with it and processing it so you can move forward again. And they are dangerous, of course, because then we need more and more to <u>keep</u> the pain away, if we are not ready, or don't ever want to, face reality.

This doesn't just apply to drinking, food or drugs—these are the ones folks may turn to in the immediate aftermath of a loss. In the long term, habits like gambling, hoarding, porn, shopping, computer games, overwork, exercise and others can arise. So while it <u>may</u> be acceptable to have a drink to get through the rough bits—stay aware and grounded in the process.

Putting Out the Fire

Friends can be very helpful in keeping you on target, in helping you with this aspect of Self-Care, as well.

But if it does go too far, don't wait—get help. . . .

A for Actions—these activities that we pursue give us the illusion that we are DOING something—we are GOING out (for drinks), we are GOING to the casino, we are GETTING more cookies and ice cream—but in fact, these past-times are keeping us from spending our time and energy doing what has to be done, and then mourning our loved one. They act as a dam for our true and authentic emotions, and therefore, they also block our healing.

R and P—to Relieve Pain—We may race around trying to spend time and energy in any way we can think of—except what we need to do to face the realities before us. The pain is so great, we cannot bear it—but **in fact, the pain comes from avoiding and denying our pain, instead of facing it**. A drink, pill or hit may indeed dull your senses for a time—a long time—but when you recover, your pain will still be there—the faithful attendant, awaiting your attention. It does not go away, it does not hide—it will arise again and again—until we decide—with intention—to face it.

So though you may find yourself having a drink to steady your nerves, don't get blitzed before the funeral—that memory will stick with you. And it will not set a good precedent for the healing work that will need to happen later. **Avoid the TARP Trap**, and keep your feet on the ground for the long term.

I had a client I will call Liz—she lost her brother in an accident, and went into a total tailspin. She called me fairly well into her second bottle of wine, the night before the funeral, where she had to give the eulogy. Her brother had been her best friend and she was just shattered. She was upset because the alcohol wasn't helping and she couldn't think of anything to write for the tribute. I told her three things—go drink a huge glass of water—wash your face—then tell me three wonderful things about your brother. We talked about him, and how central he had been to her world. She promised to honor him by speaking from the heart and staying clear-headed the next day. She called me a few days later, glad that she had created a lovely memory, rather than an awkward one. We still talk on occasion, and she is doing quite nicely.

Faith: Whatever path you follow, this is an excellent time to lean on it. I have found that people who may not be particularly observant find great comfort in their faiths of origin for ways to honor the departed. If you feel called to pray, go to church or synagogue, meditate, light candles, do it—do whatever rituals give you comfort. Connection to God/Goddess or Spirit/The Universe will help in the days and months to come. If you do not feel inclined in this direction, that is, of course, just fine, as well.

Your feelings about faith may also shift entirely—an Atheist may become religious, or a religious person may lean away from their faith. There is no right or wrong way that this happens. Your psyche and being are under stress and shifts may occur and it is ALL ok.

My father went into deep mourning after my stepmother died in 2006—he did every Orthodox mourning ritual—he didn't shave, he wouldn't wear leather shoes, he said the Kaddish (prayer for the dead) every day and night for a year, the mirrors remained covered for many months. He said it made him feel like he was honoring her.

And that's what this entire sections is about—honoring your Self and your Self-Care, and therefore, your loved one. You need to be functional and present, as decisions need to be made fairly quickly. You need your feet under you, your mind working and your spirit cared for. Fainting from hunger serves no one. Food—Water—Sleep—Breath—Faith—these will support you and are not inconveniences that you can ignore. So before we go any further—have you eaten? Go grab a bite. I'll wait, no worries.

Taking Care of Business

Anticipate the difficult by managing the easy.
                                    Lao Tzu

This falls into two categories: your immediate concerns in terms of funeral, burial, family notifications and mourning; and the business end of things in terms of the estate and belongings of the deceased.

When my mother died, we had been estranged for over two years. I had no idea of her will, arrangements, wishes or needs. Luckily, our estates attorney was an expert and helped me navigate the waters—she had a will, but had no burial plot nor had she left any instructions. I had to figure out the funeral plans, just taking a wild guess, in a very fractured state of mind and heart. I did the best I could.

And sometimes that's all we can do.

Overall, in terms of funeral and burial, my advice would be to listen to your gut. Get very quiet and really tune in to what your heart says. You will not make perfect decisions, and that is just fine. Some say funerals are for the living, which I believe to be partly true, for they are also to honor those who have passed. Think about their favorite things, songs, poems and people, if they have not told you in advance. Some people do not want a doleful and heavy service that is tough to sit through—some want a celebration, filled with stories, jokes and songs. Again, laughter can be great medicine, and bring connection and healing. Remember, there is no "wrong way," I believe. You may get indignant stares or rude comments about something being "inappropriate"— but again, do not let anyone negative or dismissive turn you from something your heart is telling you (within reason).

A competent funeral director will be able to help you with most of your practical concerns and get you extra help on details. Order extra copies of the death certificate, just in case. And if you get overwhelmed in their office and start sobbing, that's fine. They are used to it and they will wait. **If they are not compassionate, seek elsewhere for your support.**

Now just a few words about the legal bits. *I will say again, I am not an attorney and this is not to be considered legal advice in any way, shape or form.* These are just practical tips that I found useful after managing the arrangements for my family.

Don't throw any paperwork out—you might feel the urge to start tackling that huge filing cabinet or pile of unopened mail. Please don't worry about that now. Let the dust settle and the immediate needs of the funeral and mourning pass. You also don't want to toss anything that you may find out later was really important. Bills will need to be straightened out, taxes paid, credit cards canceled, etc.—but not today. Stay focused on what needs to happen right in this moment and the papers will still be there—when you are rested and more attentive, and when you can get some help.

Find the Will—and other important paperwork, but the will is most important, in case there are funeral, burial or other instructions contained there. You also need to know if there was a pre-arranged funeral that was paid for. Don't worry about anything else right at this moment.

Hire an Estates Attorney—do not go to an attorney who does not specialize in this area, as there are many layers of legalities, tax implications and paperwork that are constantly changing. Your first cousin's real estate lawyer or your neighbor's sister's divorce lawyer are not a good choice. Even if you just meet with an attorney for an hour to answer questions, that will be helpful. There are actions you will have to take later to close out your loved one's business, and it is a huge headache if these are not handled properly.

That's all—in the initial days, there is nothing else that you have to address. Turn your focus to your Self-Care, your family and friends and the task at hand. Keep breathing.

Other Major Decisions

Oh, my gosh, mom is gone and where is dad going to live and how is he going to get along without her and will he keep driving and what if he gets dementia and what happened to her china set and . . . . !!!!!

Hold on—slow down.

Breathe.

This is a terrible time to make big decisions! There are often many changes that need to be addressed in terms of moving, selling a house, parting with belongings, and family arrangements. But you cannot, and should not, make these decisions immediately. Your mind is foggy and your spirit is ungrounded, and you cannot make considered, wise choices right now. Put

Claire M. Schwartz

it aside and don't stress about it. If others try to force discussions about the china or money (I had this happen, too), ask them to wait until the dust has settled—if they are rude or persistent, have someone else explain that this is NOT the time. This leads us to our next topic. . . .

Behavior of Others

The Good, the Bad, and the Ugly

> *A real friend is one who walks in when the rest of the world walks out.*
> **Walter Winchell**

This is a huge category, with many layers to it. The folks you keep around you during these immediate hours and days can be your rock and your salvation, so you must choose them carefully. On the other hand, family and friends can be very loving and well-intentioned—right before they say something terribly hurtful. So I am going to tell you what to listen to, what sorts of folks to have around and what to do when those hurtful words coming flailing at you—because they will.

Putting Out the Fire

In my experience, the people around you following a loss or Major Life Change will fall into three categories:

1. Grounded listeners who support you, let you cry or talk or be inappropriate, and who do not impose their will on what they think you "should" do;
2. People who mean well and want to help, but end up saying hurtful or unhelpful things simply out of ignorance, but not out of malicious intent;
3. People who are so self-involved that they make your loss all about them, creating drama, imposing their ideas, taking over and talking all about themselves.

So let's start with the positive. I could not have gotten through those four days following my mother's death if not for my friends who drove me around; my dear friend Mary, whom I called at 2am that night because she had recently lost *both* her parents; my friend Beth who took me to the mall the night before my mother's funeral because I suddenly realized that I had nothing appropriate to wear; the friends in my theatre production who were so patient with me as I flew apart at the seams....

What did they all have in common?

- ➤ They listened to what I needed, rather than imposing what THEY thought should be done.
- ➤ They were patient with my craziness, knowing that I could not wrap my head around what was a good idea and what might have been a bit nuts. They let me be nuts and didn't judge.
- ➤ They were naturally empathetic, without trying to advise, push or change my grief. They met me where I was, emotionally and spiritually.

These are the folks you want around you, who will listen and support. They are naturally grounded and can put their own issues aside in order to champion your needs. They will:

- ➤ Respect your personal space and not impose.
- ➤ Let you express whatever emotions you have, without criticism or judgment.
- ➤ Keep an eye out for what is needed and volunteer to do it, rather than constantly asking, "What can I do?" Grievers are often emotionally drained and scattered—they may not know what they need.
- ➤ Make suggestions of how to help, and ask, "Would that be helpful?" rather than taking something out of your hands.

Putting Out the Fire

> ➢ Do phone calls, run errands, coordinate cooking and cleaning—all CAN be useful, as long as your responses are heard and honored.

If someone close to you seems eager to help, but they are somewhat missing the mark, it might be possible to suggest that they respond as above. These issues are painful and awkward to figure out and they may need to be told. That's fine, as long as they respect your wishes, rather than starting an argument.

On the other hand. . . .

There are probably going to be lots of folks who mean well, who don't know what to say, who are deeply uncomfortable, and end up saying the first thing that leaps into their head. They want to help—they feel the need to say something—and yet. . . .

There are going to be times when your heart is very vulnerable and a well-meaning relative will kindly put their arm around you, look you in the eye . . . and say something incredibly painful. WHAT??? Did she really say that??? You are shocked, hurt, angry— definitely NOT helpful.

So what can you say under these circumstances? It really depends on what was said, who said it, where it was said . . . and how you personally wish to deal with it. It may be possible to say, "I'm not sure that's what I had in mind" or perhaps, a very honest "that actually is not helpful", but that can also make situations worse. You might try having a designated friend as a buffer and protector who can get you out of the situation by excusing you or asking a question that will steer you away from this incident. For people who will simply not stop, pick a phrase and repeat it once or twice—"that doesn't work for me, but thanks anyway," then excuse yourself—"I have to go check on my sister."

I truly believe that this category of loved ones does not mean anything malicious. They are just echoing what our culture has taught them—most of which does not help, and makes the awkward moments even worse.

This is why I have compiled **The Ten Tall Tales of Grief and Loss**™. They are misunderstandings, misrepresentations and missteps that pretty much all of us have heard. I have based this list on a combination of things that people get told when a loss occurs, as well as the unrealistic and damaging goals of grieving that our culture teaches us, and they show themselves repeatedly.

1. *Time Heals All Wounds*

This is my Number One least favorite thing we get taught!! Time is so important to our healing, but it is

Putting Out the Fire

a question of **How** we use that time. **Waiting does not Magically Help**, in fact, it can make it worse, as your pain can be drawn out for years and decades. My touchstone for this is my favorite uncle. I love him dearly, but he always seems so melancholy—and angry—and he won't talk about it. He holds a tremendous amount of anger and resentment towards his mother (my grandmother) and has never been able to let go of it—because he has never been taught how. And she has been dead over 35 years. Even in years of therapy, no one has told him things that actually work, and he was unable or unwilling to shift his beliefs. He has carried that pain for decades, until his back is literally stooped. Time has done him no good at all.

Only Taking Action shifts you into Healing and Integration—There is no timeline for healing—the one thing I can tell you for sure is that just waiting for the pain to go away will keep you sad and stuck. Taking active healing steps, talking about your pain and your losses, working on your emotions, no matter how scary they are, is what will allow your pain to lift. It IS doable—I've walked that path—the key word is DO—and I can help you DO your healing work and bring you relief, once the immediate stuff is out of the way.

But again, in these early days, put aside your worries about how long this will take—just get through these first challenging tasks, then let yourself breathe for a bit. Begin your Healing Work mindfully and with support.

2. I Know How You Feel

Even if you have had the same loss, you do <u>not</u> know my pain because you are not Me. Folks who have also lost a parent could not even tell me what to do because they had not walked my path—even Mary, who I called at 2am that night, just sent me huge hugs and said I <u>would</u> get through it (and took my calls for months to come). So even though folks might think this helps, they can't really know your feelings and pain. Plus there is the added layer (or layers) of challenging, painful, estranged or traumatic relationships, bringing complex feelings that they may not know anything about.

Some folks may approach you and say, "Oh, I know how you feel, I lost my cousin or my neighbor . . ." and then they may often proceed to talk about themselves, rather than listening to you. This just comes from their own nervousness and discomfort about the subject. Every loss is completely personal and individual, and most folks who have been through enough loss will know this.

3. Follow the Stages of Grief

Unfortunately, the Stages of Grief written by Elizabeth Kubler Ross back in 1969 are still the only thing most people know about the process of grief. In fact, she wrote them on the subject of terminally ill patients, and not for Grievers at all. Her ideas were taken out of context and applied to grief and loss—and then used as a model for how to recover. Dr. Kubler-Ross herself in her later years tried to explain that she had been misunderstood and that the Stages should not be used for this purpose—but I'm not so sure the message has gotten through to most of our culture.

But don't we experience those emotions—denial, anger, bargaining, depression and acceptance—when we grieve? Well, maybe—as I have said, grief and mourning are deeply personal and individual. You may go through loss—and each loss over time—very differently.

Grieving and Mourning are also not linear—you don't go through periods in a nice orderly fashion, always in the same order. Emotions will change as the years rise and fall through different periods of your life and is very fluid. The Stages also imply that when you reach acceptance, you are somehow DONE with your journey, when in fact, as was my case with losing Mom, and every other major loss of my life, I have found that there is no such End Point. And that's ok. It's not about reaching The End—it's about not making your pain the entire focus of your world, and making an active, conscious decision to move forward—learning to manage what I call **Riding the Wave**—there will be ups and downs, and you will triumph as best you can. Over time, we are better served by the goal of weaving the loss in to the landscape of our lives, because it is now part of our story, our history—a chapter that will always be there.

4. Just Keep Busy

It's true, one should get some normal tasks back into life, but again, you must not deny the emotional needs that you have. Work will give you something to do—but it is an illusion and will not heal anything if you do not actively attend to your healing. It simply pushes aside your emotional needs, pain and truth, and postpones the work you have to do. Your pain is real and you deserve to have it honored.

Now I am not suggesting you shut down, stay in bed and stop living for months at a time (like I did). One must balance work with healing—going to a group, talking to a grief coach, sharing memories of a loved

Putting Out the Fire

one who has passed, building a memorial or taking on a project to honor the deceased. There is also taking care of oneself in terms of food, sleep, exercise and any medication you might need.

But if you go back to work as a way to bury your feelings, as a way of denying what has happened, it will usually backfire on you! Those emotions do not go away really—they may be out of your conscious mind for a while, but they will resurface in other ways when we push them away.

5. Isolation

This is the opposite of Just Keep Busy! Again, emotional truth will still be there when you step back out into the world. Feeling alone after a loss can be greatly magnified by isolation. It is human contact, compassionate support and friends that are so very important, especially in times of suffering. Isolation can take two forms: either the Griever isolates him/herself, or those around them tell others to leave them alone, because they just need time to be by themselves.

Self-separation may be happening for several reasons, either because the Griever may feel embarrassed by their emotions or needs, since we are taught not to have them, or maybe because they feel like they are imposing their intense feelings on those around them.

Now, different people heal and cope in different ways. For some, you may need a period to keep your feelings private—you want to have those deep sobs by yourself and just not have to worry about prying eyes. You may feel self-conscious about the intensity of your feelings, whether they be sadness, anger, confusion or even relief. And sometimes being by yourself can allow you to release those emotions, which can be healthy.

But it is a tricky balance between that and isolation. You could be cutting yourself off from the support and resources that facilitate healing. Finding a supportive community and taking Active Steps to Heal is what will open the heart again.

6. Get a Replacement

"You can just get another one," is what many folks get told after a loss. This comment may be said to someone who has gone through divorce, job loss, had a home destroyed due to accident or catastrophe. And you CAN buy a house, get a job or find love again—but this remark doesn't honor the pain that is caused by these changes.

That pain cannot be denied, dismissed or diminished by replacement—I know, I've tried. And the person saying this to you may very well think they are making you feel better. . . . But the unrest, panic and heartbreak associated with these major changes must be processed and addressed the same as any loss.

But when someone has lost a partner or a child, the idea that you can "just" get pregnant again or get married again is spectacularly insensitive. I truly hope you have not experienced this. It is often said right after a loss, when someone might be fishing for something to say and this flies out. But regardless of the timing, it deeply devalues your loved one, as if they were a spare tire you can just swap out. This loss has to be honored and addressed so healing can take place—and then you will make whatever decision is best for you going forward in your life.

This comment is also heard when one has lost a treasured animal friend (I don't even like the word "pet"—sounds too much like property) But one's lifelong companions are not trading cards or disposable commodities. They are God's creatures and members of the family. Their loss can be just as devastating and grieving for them is no less valid than grieving for a human.

7. Should's and Shouldn'ts

Plenty of people will offer a never-ending assortment of opinions about what you Should or Should Not do or have done, especially surrounding a death—about disconnecting life support, putting a pet to sleep, the funeral, the will, a memorial and so much more.

You may get disapproval, staring, whispered remarks—and this type of judgment is painful whether it is conducted to your face or behind your back.

My own experience with this was at my mother's funeral. It is Jewish tradition that the funeral not have flowers or that there be any ostentation, and that the body be entombed in a pine box. But my mother had been an elegant woman in her youth, and as she grew older, her appearance grew worse and worse—poor clothes and ill-kempt—and I could not send her on her journey with so little style and dignity. I buried her in a mahogany casket, covered with roses. I got the hairy eyeball from more than one cousin . . . I said, tough! I felt good about honoring her with something gorgeous, which she never would have done for herself.

Take care when listening to harsh commentary. It really is about doing what you feel at this moment in time. Remember, you will not make perfect decisions, and that's just fine. Again, do the best you can. Funeral practices are becoming a bit more flexible in terms of allowing celebrations of a person's life, and some may find this "inappropriate." That isn't really about you, but about their own discomfort.

This also includes folks who try and delegitimize your pain, implying that you "should" not be sad because your loved one's pain is over and they no longer suffer. You will feel the pain of the loss nonetheless. And of course, there is also the position that you "should" be over a loss by now. . . .

These are layers of guilt and shame that you do not need. Keep people around you who will help you make decisions and support you, not criticize and judge you. Grieving is deeply personal and each loss is unique. Listen to things that serve you and move you towards healing, and reach out for help when you need it.

These last three are interconnected and extremely important.

8. *There's Nothing I Can Do*

It's that helpless feeling in the pit of your stomach—when a loss hits you right between the eyes and the floor falls away. I have often had this experience when The Phone Call comes—the one that you never see coming. Then comes a slow realization—this is happening—there is nothing I can do.

Now true, of course, the reality is, something <u>has</u> happened that has shifted your life, and that cannot be changed. This person or animal has died, or this job is over, or this relationship is gone. And that feeling of helplessness is totally normal and understandable.

BUT—you are 100% in control of how you face that change.

People stay stuck in their pain and their suffering because they have been taught that they will always be helpless, and that they just have to "get through it" and deal with it. But then no healing takes place, and the feelings that need to be expressed stay within, buried and toxic—sometimes for decades.

Sometimes the pain seems so intense and so insurmountable that we can't even talk about it—what's the point? This is never going to go away, no matter how much I talk. I know that feeling all too well. . . . and then I discovered that keeping those feelings inside was making me sick—sick in my soul and sick in my life. And I found that when I did talk about it, the pain did ease. Keeping back those powerful emotions takes SO much energy, it's exhausting. It may eventually overwhelm you and explode when you least expect it.

What I advise people is to take baby steps—confide in a supportive friend, or a stranger, if that makes it easier—give yourself permission to sob uncontrollably for a spell—just once. Sharing with a compassionate person who will not judge can be very healing—and crying (or laughing, for that matter) releases endorphins that bring about a happy feeling of satisfaction. I encourage you to make a step today—then you can make the choice to start getting your life back.

Healing IS doable—I know because I have done it and continue to do it. And many others have, too.

9. Getting Over or Getting Past the Loss

This implies that someday, you will forget your loved one who passed, which of course, you will never do. There will never be a time that your spouse, child, friend or companion will just disappear. But that does not mean that you must think of them every minute of every day, buried in your grief for the rest of your life. Honoring them does not mean sacrificing your own happiness—and your loved one would not want that for you. You can honor them by creating good in your life—giving their belongings away to those in need, using your journey to help others or making a donation in their memory.

This remark also implies there is an End Point to Grief and Loss, when you will someday just be "Over it." But what really happens is that you do get **better** and you learn how to live with the hole this has been created.

Let me tell you what I have done with the loss of my mother and the hole it left in my life and spirit. During that summer when I had my nervous breakdown,

Claire M. Schwartz

I began to have a recurring dream—I was standing in blackness, nothing above me and nothing below or around me. Just one thing—a deep dark hole, which I knew was the loss of my mother. That's it—that was the whole dream—standing there staring at this big hole.

But in the following years, as I learned more about Mom, read her letters and her poetry, I started to heal and I began to grow older—the hole changed. I placed a short white picket fence around it, maybe three inches high. In the spring, I would plant around it—she loved petunias. I planted a peony bush, her favorite—and bulbs that would bloom every year—a small tree. The air is always fragrant with floral scents. There is now a cobblestone path curving around the hole, and winding in front of it. And I have a stone bench where I sit—where Mom and I can visit. Now it is usually warm and spring-like—and I can talk to her anytime. The hole is still there—it cannot be filled. But it is not a foreboding hopeless place anymore.

People can be very dismissive of your loved one's life and also your emotional pain, usually saying, "you JUST need to get past this," or worse, "haven't you gotten over that yet?" You WILL get through this and step into the Light again—if you take active steps to work on it.

10. When Will I Feel Normal Again?

I told you how I asked my friend about when I would get back to my Normal—and I continue to hear this from many Grievers during the beginning stages. But the fact is that the goal doesn't make sense in the first place.

And what I have realized over the years is that I was reaching for something that could not happen. I could not go back to life before my mother died—those times were gone. My Normal had **moved**—and one has to adjust, learn, heal and keep going. My healing process began to be finding who I was after this life-changing event—and this has been true for every one of the major losses I have had since then, including my father and stepmother, my childhood home, my elderly cats and my job.

A better goal, in other words, is to learn how to weave the loss into your life story. This loss will permanently become part of the narrative of who you are. It is a process of exploration, introspection and reinvention—and it is a marathon, not a sprint. But it is doable—and it is also essential—as we make sure that we are shaped by our losses, and not reduced by them.

There are SO many more things that have been taught, or we get told—some of them are so deeply cruel,

I cannot fathom saying them to another human being. But in each of the ones I address in my **Ten Tall Tales of Grief & Loss**™, I explain their fallacy and give you more empowering and useful things to focus on.

As Brené Brown, the sociologist and revolutionary author of *Daring Greatly; How the Courage to be Vulnerable Transforms the Way We Live, Love, Parent, and Lead* reminds us, Change takes Courage—and you cannot have Courage and Comfort at the same time. That does mean stepping into the unknown, and that can be uncomfortable. But it is much more preferable than sitting in the soup of despair the rest of your days.

It is about building a New Normal, based on this new reality, learning what it is like in this place where this person, place or thing is no longer in your life. How we navigate change is one of the most important things to learn for our journey. And yes, you CAN.

Getting back to how others may respond, I just briefly want to touch on certain circumstances surrounding a death may cause extra judgments to arise:

- Illnesses where it is perceived that the deceased did not take care of themselves.
- Deaths due to addiction to drugs or alcohol.
- AIDS
- Suicide

More guilt and shame here—and the things that folks can say when the above occurs can be particularly disparaging and harsh. I have personally heard so many mean and terrible things said after the death of an addict, or after someone dies too young who was overweight and stressed and smoking.

There is little one can do stop hurtful comments—try to insulate yourself from these folks and surround yourself with loving, supportive others. Know that there is compassion and care available from more open hearts. Sadly, this does not apply to everyone.

Vultures and Vampires. Finally, there is category of people who truly are only about <u>themselves</u>. They may lecture you—they may deride you or constantly criticize your choices, they may try and take over—or they may constantly talk about their own losses and how terrible their pain is. Their neediness will drain you like a vampire or their need to be the center of attention and be in charge will gnaw at you like a vulture.

Death, funerals, wills and the like tend to bring out the best in some people, and the worst in others. May your time with the latter be brief. But if/when you find yourself confronted with such an individual, they can either be maneuvered out of the situation or, if they actively interfere, they need to have things taken out of their hands and kept away from the Griever. Hopefully, they will not do irreparable damage and are, at the very least, annoying. Focus on the loving support of folks who listen and are strong and grounded. They are your allies and your advocates.

Keep in mind that family tensions, old wounds and rivalries may come to the surface during this intensely emotional period. Battles can erupt about who should have done what, who gets what in the will, lots of indignation and resentment. Now is not the time. Gently remind people that this is a time for honoring the deceased and expressing our sorrow. There is plenty of time for pettiness later. Take a deep breath.

Remember, too, that different family members will have different memories and experiences of the deceased. They are all valid and true, as each person's experience is their own. But again, in the first few days may not be the best time to address those, when emotions are high and so many heightened decisions have to be made. There will be plenty of time for coaching and counseling, too—later.

So in these hours and days full of so much immediacy and vulnerability, keep these three things at hand when dealing with the Behavior of Others:

1. Keep the folks around you who listen, who get it and who support you.

Putting Out the Fire

2. Put hurtful comments in their proper context—folks are usually not being mean, they just don't know what to say.
3. If truly negative people show themselves and interfere, gently remove them from the situation, or remove yourself.

You WILL get through these first tough days—seek your allies, block out the rest.

Time & The Longer Term

Mastery is Nine Times Patience.
Ursula K. LeGuin

The concept of Time around a Major Loss is something I see covered in few other venues. Especially in these first days when the loss is fresh, time can get very WEIRD, for lack of a better word. First there is the change in the passage of time. This can take several different forms:

> ➢ One's ability to sense the passage of time can become completely off. You may not be sure how much time has passed in terms of hours. You may feel like time has become so sluggish, that you cannot believe that only two days have passed since the funeral, for instance.

Putting Out the Fire

➤ You may feel like eating or sleeping at odd times of the day—or night.
➤ You may have the sensation of going through quicksand—everything is slower—slower—sllllooooowwwerrrrrr. . . .

All of these perceptions are completely normal—you are probably operating in a low state of shock that will wear off in a few days. Just take a deep breath, honor how you feel. Again, even if it feels strange, do remember to eat and sleep—you need fuel and rest. And ask others to help you.

Now there can also be a second level of S-L-O-W later on, just so you know, where you get stuck in that phase where Time is Weird—that may go on for months. But I encourage you to keep processing, keep feeling, keep actively working on your healing as you are able. When/If you feel your grief taking over, reach out to a grief coach, support group, close friends and those you feel will be empathetic. You may need to take breaks—this is tough stuff. But staying engaged in your healing will lighten your load and ease your transition.

Overwhelm. You have SO much to do and you may feel like you are drowning in details at a time when your emotions are raw and your resources are burnt out. Time in this instance can create pressure and stress, because there are deadlines and so many things to manage.

Here is a key piece of advice for getting through this whole process:

You only have to manage One Minute at a Time.

That's right—break it down—when time is moving SO slowly, hearing that you just need to take things a day at a time can feel excruciating—a whole DAY??? That can feel like forever. But all you have to handle is **One Minute.** You can do it, I know you can.

> Take another Deep Breath.
> Count out ten seconds—one, two, three, four. . . .
> Take it slow, you're in no rush.
> Good for you, you got to 10!
> Bravo!
> Another deep breath.
> You can manage that—it feels manageable.
> Just that tiny bit, is all you have to do.

You are allowed to let your emotions out in that time, too. Cry, rage, scream, pound the floor.

Then when you are done, you will have given yourself permission—to FEEL—to BE—to only be able to cope with One Minute. That's fine. More than fine, that's excellent. Give yourself credit for getting through that minute. Now you are ready to take on the next.

And yes I am aware that wasn't a minute—doesn't matter. The point is, you only have to manage each bit as you are able. I sure wish someone had told me that all those years ago. . . .

Foreseen or Sudden. In my experience, it does not matter if a loved one's death was a long time coming from an illness or from an accident—you will still have the reality hit you when they are, in fact, gone. You are still entitled to your pain and the need to Mourn. This goes back to what others may tell you—"but you knew this was coming, right?" As if that mitigates your sense of loss or what you are "allowed" to feel. Not having that person there in Real Time can change everything, no matter how prepared you thought you were. And that is totally fine—again, you are entitled to say you are—and be—in pain.

Here is another truth I have learned from my journey—there is only one way that seeing a death coming can be a bit easier than a sudden one. If you are lucky, you may be able to have those conversations—clear the air—apologize and forgive—share memories—honor last requests—these times can be a tremendous gift. If your family dynamic allows it so, you may wish to take advantage of those times. Say what needs to be said.

Claire M. Schwartz

As a poignant example I'd like to share with you the story of my amazing stepmother, Eva Klein. She won our hearts immediately with her intelligence, her kindness and her grace of spirit, even though my mother had only been gone two years when she married my father. It was an extraordinary period of my life, feeling more like a family than I had experienced growing up. There was still dysfunctional of course (what family is perfect?), but we went on trips, shared recipes and I learned a great deal from her. It took extraordinary courage to uproot her life in Israel, give up her country and prominent career, and to come join us in the US, solely because she wanted that family.

But after only five years with us, she told us her breast cancer had returned. Misdiagnosed for over a year, it was now the size of a grapefruit and inoperable. Her treatments began immediately and they ravaged her entire being. The manner in which my stepmother approached her ending was heroic—after three years (yes, I said years . . .) of chemo and radiation on her massive breast cancer invasion, she was worn out. She lost weight and looked deflated. When it became clear that she was not going to leave the hospital, my poor heartbroken father could only sit by her bedside, already numb. I asked what she wanted, and I made it my business to move mountains to make sure she had it. She wanted to talk to the hospital's attorney about how the staff didn't listen to her—a lawyer was by her side within the hour. She wanted to talk to someone in power about healthcare for children with no insurance in this country—I made that happen, too. After she moved to the hospice wing, she called her friends all over the world to say goodbye—in several languages—then she called her brother, whom she had not told that she was ill. After she finished the last call, she looked at my father and me—and gave us, shall we say, a good talking to . . . about taking care of each other. She then ordered me back to New York from Michigan to finish my two years of training as a Reiki Master—I said I would go, if she could wait for me. "I'll be here," she said. "OK—now I rest." I flew back that night—and she died in dawn's hour the next morning. Eva's extraordinary story is one of the most inspirational things I have ever witnessed, and she is one of the reasons I do healing work.

And yet even after all of that, there was much that was left unsaid between us—there always is. But I am still so very grateful that I could be there for her and be her advocate in her final hours. She taught me priceless lessons—and I am indebted to her and to her memory.

Rules of Time. At some point, maybe a year or more, someone may ask you, "aren't you over that yet?" Overall, I would say that no one is allowed to dictate to you how long you stay brokenhearted or how you "should" be healing. Do not listen to those who would lecture you on this.

HOWEVER—when the grieving takes over and is the main thing in your life, changes may need to be considered. So how long should we allow ourselves to grieve?

This is a tricky answer. And it is a matter of degree and what is healthy, which, again, our society does a poor job of teaching us. So I am going to share what I have learned.

Healthy—crying, raging and expressing one's heartache and confusion.

Unhealthy—doing this for months on end, not leaving the house.

Healthy—understanding that your health will go wonky for a while—this lasted about three months for me, eating odd things, having nightmares, poor sleep habits, etc.

Unhealthy—letting it get to the point where you do permanent damage to your health.

Healthy—allowing a TARP to ease the pressure of the moment, having a drink before delivering the eulogy, or taking a pill to sleep. **NOTE:** if you already know that you are prone to addiction, do NOT tread in

Putting Out the Fire

dangerous waters—get extra support, go to meetings every day, call your sponsor, whatever you need to do to stay sober and healthy.

Unhealthy—falling into addictive behavior to subvert our pain and emotions—this applies to drinking, drugging, gambling, shopping or anything else that begins to take over your life. Again, get help <u>immediately</u>.

And here are some signs that you may be pushing the envelope on time:

- ➤ Your house is un-cleaned for weeks at a time.
- ➤ You stop showering for more than a week.
- ➤ You are spending more time drunk than sober.
- ➤ Your children are acting out because you are unavailable to them and/or their own grieving and mourning has not been attended to.
- ➤ You isolate yourself in your house.

These are times when you need to take a serious look at getting more support in moving forward. This will likely be slow and painstaking, so it is VERY important that you get good assistance, good resources and get to know your life as it now stands.

I imagine that may sound like being overwhelmed all over again. But it IS doable. This is still Your Life—it has changed—perhaps permanently. But you can find your way on this new path. It took many years for me, because I did not have the resources that I bring to you. I hope to support you in this process and want you to know that there is LIGHT out there for you! Don't live in the Dark.

The Longer Term—Just to reemphasize: there is a lot of misconception out there about the idea that grief is linear—that we go through Kubler-Ross's stages in a certain order, and then we are DONE. I have found there is nothing about this that is true or helpful. As time passes, you will relive certain stages, jump around, feel a shift perhaps at one year, five years, ten years . . . there really is no rhyme or reason to it—and that is <u>fine</u>. I find it more helpful to think of the process as a wave, rather than a straight line.

The expectation that this has changed you is much more realistic than the one that tells you that you are going to Get Past This or Be Done With That. So as years pass, your relationship to the loss will change with you. It becomes a part of you and you learn how to integrate it into your Life Story.

At the end of this book, I have a section called Resources, which outlines ways you can access all the ways in which I can support you on your healing journey, including my blog, classes, book and more.

Celebrating Your Loved One and Yourself

The personal life deeply lived always expands into truths beyond itself.

Anais Nin

So let's bring some positivity back into this process. It is so important to your healing that if you have lost someone with whom you had an important and loving relationship, be it family, friend, animal or stranger, that you express your emotions and honor them. Here are several things you may plan in the short term to give voice to your pain and memories.

- Take flowers to the grave site, memorial site, or other place where you go to remember your loved one.

Putting Out the Fire

- Make a digital photo album on a photo service, such as Mixbook, Shutterfly or others, and give it as a gift to others who loved them, or keep one for yourself as memento.
- Light memorial candles.
- Visit a favorite place of your loved one, or a place that reminds you of them.

In Jewish tradition, sitting shiva is the period following the funeral where family and friends gather to support loved ones and share stories about the deceased. In Catholic tradition, a wake often serves the same function before a funeral, with a repast (meal) following the funeral. These both can devolve into social events where cell phones and mingling take priority. But if you can keep the focus on remembering and sharing, these can have deep value. Using this as an opportunity for leaning on one another and reconnecting is an excellent use of these traditions.

I know these are common things—I know these are simple things—and that's totally fine—more ideas will come to you later when you can think more clearly. That's enough to think of right now. I have more ideas listed in the Conclusion of this book. It will give you ideas that are positive, life-affirming and put the focus on ways to honor your loved one going forward, rather than just looking back.

A Toxic or Challenging Individual. Now here's some really challenging stuff. . . . If the person who has deceased was someone who was abusive, or with whom you had a difficult relationship (which I would say is more folks than people think), and honoring them doesn't sit right with you, the important thing is to honor **Yourself**.

Self-Care is the most important way of doing this:

- Get back to a regular schedule of eating, exercising, sleeping, etc.
- Get a massage.
- Take a walk out in Nature.
- Spend time with friends (the supportive, empathetic ones).
- If journaling resonates with you, write about your thoughts and feelings, even if it only makes sense to you, and even if nobody ever sees it. It can help to get those thoughts out of your head and onto paper.

And perhaps most importantly, if there are feelings of confusion, guilt, relief, anger and other complex emotions in this equation, get help in sorting them out. These are all totally normal and understandable, believe me. . . . These early days may bring an avalanche of conflicting feelings—you WILL figure them out, over time. Right now, just honor them, know that they are not wrong and promise to address them later.

Be Gentle With Yourself

This is a very challenging time, as you are reeling from the shock of your loss and all that is being thrown at you. This stuff is painful, can bring stress and worry and confusion, and you may be surprised by many things.

Being Gentle with Yourself is key—just keep in mind these simple things:

1. The goal is not to be perfect—you will do the best you can.
2. You will not make perfect decisions—that's okay.
3. Your memory will be faulty—have others support you, you'll be fine.
4. Your heart is hurting and your mind in a whirl—that's okay.
5. You are human—and humans hurt and make mistakes—and that's okay.

Keep reminding yourself of these truths in these initial times of stress.

Go back to the breathing we did at the beginning.

Take a deep breath
Close your eyes
Take a long deep breath through your nose
Inhale for 5 seconds
One—two—three—four—five
Then I want you to slowly exhale through your mouth over 5 seconds
One—two—three—four—five
Again.
A long deep breath, in through the nose, out through the mouth
Then do it again, in . . . . and out . . . .
And a final time, in . . . . and out . . . .

Breath is life—I know you feel like you may not be able to breathe. More release and more tears are perfectly fine—they will cleanse your spirit and relieve some stress.

We still good? OK. Excellent job—I'm proud of you.

Conclusion

There is a crack in everything ~
That's how the light gets in.
Leonard Cohen

So I hope this hasn't all been too much for you to absorb. I have addressed the major things that come up, keeping things simple and clear, with answers to questions that empower you and tell you the truth. You may find useful information and support here long after the initial phase has passed. I truly hope so.

You are at the beginning of a journey. Once you have gotten through the shock and the stress of the funeral and early mourning period, the situation changes. Family and friends who are not immediately impacted by this loss may go back to their lives—the phone calls may stop coming and you find yourself alone, where it is very quiet—and a new level of pain may set in—so what now?

Turn to the next phase of things that need to happen:

- ➢ Dealing with the Will and the Estate—again, make sure you get really good legal advice.
- ➢ Distribution of personal items and effects—this may cause another wave of emotion, as well as family stress. Stay grounded, keep people around you who support you and try not to get caught up in family drama.
- ➢ Do not make major decisions that you feel rushed about, unless it is absolutely necessary. If you are forced to act, get help and support.

You can also now begin to consider some of the ways you might want to remember a loved one:

- ➢ Volunteer for an organization that had meaning for them.
- ➢ Create a scholarship fund in their memory, if you are able.
- ➢ Donate to a charity that had meaning for them.
- ➢ Begin a Keepsake Box of their treasured items or things that remind you of them.

- Plant a tree in their honor.
- Plan a trip with friends and family to their favorite place and have a Story Sharing about them.
- Gather their favorite recipes and serve them to friends and family at a dinner in their honor, or have a pot luck and have them bring dishes your loved one made or liked.
- Make a memorial Photo Album of their life.

If this is someone with whom you had a challenging or toxic relationship:

- Honor yourself and take excellent care of your health.
- Journal about all the feelings that are coming up.
- Donate their personal items that bring up painful memories, so others can benefit and bring some good out of the pain.
- If the memories create more trauma, and you feel out of control, put it aside for now, or seek professional counseling.

Overall, this is the most important thing I can impart to you.

LOSS CHANGES YOU.

I will say that again.

LOSS CHANGES YOU.

You are not the same person you were before this happened. And that can be very scary, because it may not have been an event of your choosing, at a time in your life that was convenient. There is no telling who you would have been if this had not happened, or if it had happened earlier or later. There is nothing any of us can do about that.

What you CAN do something about, is what happens now. Your choices, and what you do with the tools that you learn along the way, are entirely up to you.

I am not the person I was—I am better, stronger, smarter and happier for having gone through this suffering, for it has shaped the person I am. I have more to offer my friends and family, I am no longer knocked over by every whiff of adversity that comes my way, and I have a resilience and connection to myself that I never thought possible. I continue to learn and grow every day, and I am blessed to do so.

But I didn't know any of this when I started. And I didn't have the tools or the support I needed. It took many decades to figure all this out—so now I present it to you, so that you know—KNOW—that life is still beautiful, healing is doable, and that you are stronger than you know.

Thank you so much for stepping into your healing—I wish you all the best as you move forward.

> *"Out of suffering have emerged the strongest souls; the most massive characters are seared with scars."*
>
> **~ Khalil Gibran**

Biography

Claire Schwartz was born in a suburb of Detroit to educated and cultured parents, attending one of the foremost schools in the US for gifted children for first to twelfth grade. Her formative years were turbulent and traumatic, including abuse & neglect, violence, rape and other damaging incidents. It encompassed the beginnings of what she calls The Dark Ugly™. She attended the University of Michigan, Ann Arbor, graduating in 1993 with a BA in Psychology, as she sought to figure herself out and navigate the world having had little instruction. During college, she took a semester overseas, traveling to 40 cities in 18 countries in 100 days, opening her eyes to the world outside her own pain.

The pivotal moment of her life took place in 1995 with the sudden death of her mother, causing a nervous breakdown. But she moved to New York in 1996 to pursue her acting career, determined to reinvent her life. Years and years of therapy began, as she struggled to recreate what had been taken from her. She tried careers in performing, administration and restaurants—none of which spoke to her. The light began to dawn when she took a two-year training program to become a Reiki Master Teacher—the idea of doing healing work spoke to her deeply, and echoed back to college. After living in the same apartment in Astoria, Queens for 12 years, she thought a move to New Jersey would move her towards new possibilities.

But from 2010–2012, she experienced her Avalanche of Loss—friendships, her elderly cats, her teacher, her father, her childhood home and the disastrous mess inside it, her best friend's dad—health, time, opportunities . . . it just went on and on, culminating in the loss of her oldest friend and mentor. Again seeking an answer to her own sorrows, she began studying grief and loss. Now finally she has the chance to live from her truest passion—turning her broken past into tools for others. She is happily married to her scientist and fellow geek, Mark, with multiple felines and a growing garden. She can finally breathe—having put out her own fire.

Claire M. Schwartz
BA, Spiritual Counselor, Reiki Master Teacher
Certified Professional Coach &
Grief Healing Expert
Interfaith Minister

Resources

All blog posts can be found on my website.

Eva's Story and The Ten Tall Tales of Grief & Loss™ are right at the top of my blog.

When Loss Has Just Happened

Copies of this book, *Putting Out The Fire* make compassionate gifts—everyone will have losses in their lives and need Truths & Tools to handle those initial hours and days.

The First Steps on Your Healing Journey

All the details on my 6-week classes are available on my website under **Products & Services** on my website. They are available in both group and private formats, and take place by phone.

New individual classes are being added, so bookmark that page and check back often.

All of my classes point you clearly towards finding your New Normal, putting the focus on recrafting your life and your happiness—and new teaching tools are being added all the time.

I am available for **Free ½ Hour Consultations** and you can make an appointment directly from my website. We can solve the Three Most Frustrating Things

Putting Out the Fire

that are holding you back right now to get you immediate and personal support.

Finally, email me to make an appointment privately to get personalized and unique tools for your particular situation—every loss is different, requiring personal attention and support in moving forward.

www.YouCanHealYourGrief.com

youcanhealyourgrief@gmail.com